Hit the Ground Running

Muses, reflections, poems, prayers
and rants on life's crazy journey

Hilary Jane Hughes

Onwards and Upwards Publishers

Berkeley House,
11 Nightingale Crescent,
Leatherhead,
Surrey,
KT24 6PD.

www.onwardsandupwards.org

ISBN: 978-1-907509-78-0

Cover design: Guilherme Gustavo Condeixa

About the Author

Hilary is a teacher and writer with a grown-up family. She has found her creative voice partly (but not entirely) through struggles with self-worth/identity, panic attacks, feeling punished, years of unfocussed grief in childlessness, chronic anxiety and sleeplessness! She has discovered that Christian faith does not negate or eradicate problems but gives a clear dimension beyond these things; the love that Jesus has for each person must be grasped and understood. Formerly unexpressed thoughts and emotions inform her work, sometimes directly 'involving God' and at other times indirectly, as in writing about places (particularly wilderness) and Thailand, a special place for her.

Here are fifty-five pieces, varied in length and focus. Some of her poems are raw and restless, others sentimental, whimsical or quirky and yet others a pouring out of love from the heart and from God. Who will read her work? Well, anyone who thinks and feels deeply about things, or who wants to, anyone who feels that they are never good enough, even if they are a Christian, and also those Christians who never seem to struggle with life and faith. She has tried to be real, honest and God-looking, as well as acknowledging that much of life is mysterious and crazy! Her poems have been read within a worship setting and elsewhere, and her hope is they will inspire readers to be real about themselves, to 'bash on' in faith, to own their gifts and use them for others and for the Lord.

Hilary currently lives in Yorkshire with her husband and is immensely proud of her children both of whom married in 2012!

Acknowledgements

Thanks to my long-suffering family, Mike, Dave and Joey, especially Mike, as he has witnessed the births of many of these poems.

To my dear friends, Lynn and John, in particular John, who has read and re-read my scripts making sound and sensible suggestions about how to present my work.

To Gail, Sharon and all friends and others who say they have been blessed by my writing and have encouraged me.

And to Luke Jeffery and his staff at Onwards and Upwards.

Finally, to God, who unfathomable as He is, is the source of all creative spirit.

Endorsements

If, as Wordsworth said, "Poetry is the spontaneous overflow of powerful feeling", here is poetry indeed – the passionate music of the human soul crying out. The reality of faith in these poems is a challenge to our complacent hypocrisy. They enable us to take a step forward in faith and integrity.

Colin Lake, M.A., B.D.
27th March, 2013

If you are seeking a deeper appreciation of the natural world, and of the inner world of the spirit we sometimes call our soul, then read these poems.

Hilary's descriptions of locations and scenes have a natural beauty and rhythm that bring them to life. Her poems also explore some of the hurts that life throws at us all from time to time and the possibility of God being involved in the subsequent healing process.

John Seabridge
Writer and Poet
22nd March, 2013

Hilary Hughes has a real gift for creative writing. Her use of language is arresting, vivid and thought-provoking and I warmly commend her work to you. Enjoy reading her poems – better still, read them aloud – and find yourself enfolded in a tapestry of words that will open your mind and heart to eternal truths in a fresh and exciting way.

Brian Hoare
Former President of the Methodist Conference,
Hymn Writer and Author
March, 2013

…sometimes deeply thought-provoking and hard-hitting, sometimes colourfully vivid … Hilary's poetry will set your imagination dancing as she points to a great Creator.

Suzan Robinson
Worship Leader / Songwriter
March, 2013

Contents

Wonder... 9

Pain 29

Muse 43

People... 69

Contact the Author 93

Similar Books by the Publisher 94

To all students of English as a
Foreign Language, especially Lam,
you are an inspiration! Keep up the
good work!

Wonder

Places, Weather, Creation

Here are a variety of pieces about places - cities and landscapes, home and abroad. Weather patterns, times of day and seasons all stir the creative spirit; of their nature they are from God. Haikus are a Japanese poetic form; they force the writer to be concise and focussed on the subject, using a limited number of words and syllables.

This section is largely observational but deeply evocative and moving, especially those poems written in Thailand and Yellowstone National Park, USA.

Winter Senses

step
inside frozen world of bitter cold,
gasp
and shiver as ferocity grasps you,
feel
dazzled, bewildered to extreme,
wait
stunned in soundless moment,
watch
as veils of snow rush relentlessly past,
slide
clumsily across glassy floor,
shrink
as skin tightens round bones,
carve
a place where feet can glide,
hear
numbing intensity of whiteness,
marvel
as monochrome reshaping fills time and space,
gaze
at ice kingdom disguising itself,
listen
to pounding of heartbeat,
stand
in strange but certain comfort of silence,
snowbound

Hilary Hughes

Dusk by the Chao Praya River

First trip to Thailand

A pool, lit majestically from its sides,
frames a few heads of lazy swimmers;
pleasure boat's shape etched out with
lines of bright and lavish lights, slowly sails up-river;

across the spine of this waterway that doesn't sleep,
a barge, towed with its three brothers, by a tiny tug –
masked by its mast as it ploughs downstream;
Chinese-roofed hotel shuttles pass each other,
crossing the swirling river with practised precision;

the Peninsula Hotel rises triumphantly from the
soft green-lit banks, dwarfing the grey lower buildings;
a long-tailed boat, prow lifted, and with its small dim lantern,
carves its own lane, purposefully pursuing its task;

palms sway and flicker in the variations of light
and the river's surface constantly exchanges lines
and shapes of different dimensions, sometimes parallel,
always blending, changing, closing in, expanding,

as dusk becomes dark on the Chao Praya.

Vertigo Bar

From the top of the Banyan Tree Hotel, Bangkok

From highest tower
View a
Crazy, flat-topped
Mountain range
All hung
With festive
Squares of light

Thousands
Of tiny bulbs
Pulsing and
Punctuating the dark
Plunging into
The depths
Of night

The buildings crowd
Conspiratorially together
Wrapped in
Thin ribbons of street
Where jewels slide along
Miniature necklaces
And in the distance
Familiar views
Merge into
The horizon
Hiding secrets
City life
At night

Bangkok Cafe

Sat with my Italian style coffee,
graced with a fan of serviettes
on a silver stand.
Through the glass in the small street,
twisted cables writhe away from view,
strung haphazardly from concrete posts.

Bikes, busy with rear or front carriers,
momentarily mask the flowery
jacaranda trees and stubby palms.
Street stalls, empty till later,
domed in blue plastic and topped
with flags of king and country.

Higher in my sight, bent cranes hover
over a growing condominium.
Below the skyline, facets, balconies,
air-con units stuck on like facial features.
An awkward satellite dish, angled
like a great chimney brush.

Lower, colonnades frame blue glass panes
reflecting the humid heat braved by a
slick-suited businessman in a crystal-white shirt.
Green truck rattles past, aboard,
brown-overalled men on their way to work.

Orange-coated taxi-meter, embossed with
white Thai script, obscures for a moment
a starched-hatted cook with buckets of coconut milk.
Outside the cafe, a pick-up stops and timber poles
off-loaded and stored. A young girl in slacks,
magazine covering her head, strides past the window.

And city life endures,
manically, steadily,
dreamily, crazily,
before my eyes.

By the Oriental Pool

Delicate shades of frangipane,
flowers hang together,
pink, yellow, cream, softly swaying
from spreading branches.
Strong-stemmed, deep
green leaves frame fragile ferns,
and heart-shaped plants
tremble in ornamental pots.
A powerful beauty of orchid stems,
nodding and bowing their flowery strings.
Minute raindrops prick the surface
of rippling water. Beyond,
the searing river sends barges
on their way, solemn and sedate,
while ferries slide and bob
and dodge their pathways.
Close by me, frailest petals float on
miniature waves and punctuate
conversations of tiny bubbles.

Holiday Haikus

Wales and Essex

hillside's ivy-clad gravestone –
the jackdaw and butterfly's
playing space

thin skirts of rain
each with their own light rhythm
spread their pleats across the roof

such exuberance of plants
waving orange flowers from
lane-side banks

sapphire-haloed dimples
on water's surface
sparkle in sunlight

house walls of peach,
lavender, salmon and mint
snuggle at Haven's head

pigeons' battle within the branches
scatters bright plums
on hard dry earth

September's trembling twigs
fan flamboyant leaves
in farewell to summer

Malham Cove

Breath vapour vanishes in dappled autumn sunlight,
shafting and sweeping past cove's high, high wall;
milky-grey, a parchment inscribed with short,
brave trees at intervals across rock's surface;
lines of greetings span, stretch and meet in
pale limestone layers, punctuated by grassy ledges;
two dark birds wing possessively over the cliff
against an ocean of sky, deep and consistent.
And where cove meets ground, a thousand rivulets
surge eagerly round mossy stones;
size and scale and spectacle quietly dominate
the scene, inspiration breathing.

Norfolk Haikus

Plump, pink pigeon,
swaying in spindly bush,
calculates a landing.

Clumpy green gorse,
studded with yellow blossom,
nods and sways in Spring breeze.

Sun shines through
pink ears of small rabbit,
nibbling earnestly at grass shoots.

Hilary Hughes

Snowbound, Spellbound

Scarborough to Knaresborough late at night

Deep, deep silence of snowy night,
boundaries, gradients,
foreground, background, indistinct.
No traction sound as wheels roll on icy surface;
snow shafts looming out of darkness;
silvery owl flashes in flight, then gone
as snow curtains shroud all airborne.

White-bright hills fold into themselves,
the way between honoured by crystal
branches, bending into view on either side;
we slip, we slide, then grip and hold,
keep a steady speed, peering through
vast veils towards –a distance,
masked with a million snowflakes,
melting, then freezing on cold, hard ground.

Wind takes snowfall sideways now,
then, spinning, over and over,
fading, disappearing, then constantly
rebirthing in an endless wave,
but, soundless, eerie;
menacing yet magical,
mesmerising, manic;

flakes flutter, forgetful, foreign,
now flying, then shrinking slowly,
dark diminishing them to faint flickers
as they fall, and die.
Charcoal sky chokes its last clouds of snow,
and sound returns, from the stillness,
as we journey on.

Over Greenland

Unexpected, vast, clean, pure,
sprinkled with dust of humanity
in tiny inlets like the silver clasp
of a pearl necklace;
cubes of ice floating in fiords;
mountain peaks as dark fins in a snow sea,
ridges of regular pyramids, poking through,
others as folds in a wide counterpane,
stark white at their base,
wrinkles and pleats rolling over the land,
sastrugi, swerving and rising –
a sight remembered for
its clarity, uniqueness and grace.

January Journey

Beige, bedraggled sheep, grazing on beige, crop-cut field,
rumps in shadow as the sun climbs a reluctant daily arc;

strips of wispy cloud gather in furrows above;
a surprising green-ness appears amidst the muted
winter tones, then lost in the shade of the looming cliff.

Later, a silvery smoke-spring leans across the landscape
as if painting the straggly moorland tracks.

Grouse, black and flustered and complaining,
rush about the heather; then, a perpetual roar
the only sound as we push forward, the blast
numbing our feet and fingers and our heads from thinking,
(no point in talking); a salty-smoke is inhaled and
we taste the flavour of the winter winds and head
for thick dark beer, smooth, to warm and soothe.

Togwatee Pass

On the way to Yellowstone National Park

low-slung hills with an unshaven look,
tree-lined creeks, stony cuttings,
peaks drizzled with sugar;
a grooved face leers across
alluvial moraine;

the ridge side falls away
in a skirt of cream-coloured rock;
green lines form a tartan pattern
with streaks of rusty-orange and purple;
trees and trees and trees pierce the sky
like pots of sharpened pencils;

lodges vie with pagoda-cliffs
to stripe the canyon;
tubes of grey lower themselves
from the hillside, the jagged
becoming rounder now, and safe
for buffalo to wander in;

log fences in a zigzag meander
deter deer and cattle; like the
spines of an ancient dinosaur,
more stone ledges reach down
to the river as giant stalactites;

silver-grey dead branches, cold-gnawed,
heat-killed or beetle-eaten, hang
beside a trunk, like the
withered arms of an old crone.

Hilary Hughes

Geothermal Yellowstone –
Fire and Water Meet

Before the mountain ranges, studded with lodgepole pines,
and soft, blue skyscape crowned, spread strange and eerie sights,
hidden in mists of steam, then slowly and curiously revealed.

Beneath the surface, the pulse of heat and rock and boiling mighty
    power,
ready in their own time to explode, amaze and tantalise!
Imagine the force below, dictating when and where each
spring and geyser vents, and how, incredibly, imperceptible
microorganisms survive and flourish in the sizzling heat,
producing vibrant colours, greens and turquoises;

crusty minerals frill the fumaroles; amber, ochre,
glowing, glinting in the day's brightness; their crystal
crenulations belie a sinister secret of dark and dangerous
activity; beside them, clear, calm pools of unknown depths,
from which curl golden tendrils, reaching out as rays
of sunlight;

mudpots are turbulent and bubbling,
mocha-like, sulphurous and odorous; then comes
the roaring, like some approaching monstrous steam
engine, from Dragon's Mouth; a vast volume of water
rises, pushed above by weighty rock and air, and
shoots, high and fast, escaping from its confines, in a
wild, extravagant display, like water fireworks!

Travertine terraces, shiny, ever-changing, sculpted
through the years, limestone and water creating
chalky-white hills and pools and stalagmite folds;
seething heat and water-gas combine in such
immensity and charm, to inspire and thrill the
wondering crowds;

and still at night the landscape
fizzes and streaks across the setting sun and on
till morning, when another day in a kind of
alien paradise erupts and entices us again.

Chama RV Park after the Train

Now when I close my eyes,
even though I'm sitting still
under the cedar trees,
I'm moving slowly, steadily
along a ledge on the side
of a mountain; across the gorge
are lines of firs and aspen,
like soldiers ready to march;

far below, beneath the rock pillars,
slides a stream, visible for a moment.
I open my eyes and I'm sitting
still under the cedars;
my mind and body tell me I'm here,
but once more with eyes shut tight,
I shudder and shift as the wheels grip
the rails, wipe specks of dust from
my face and breathe in the steam
as it evaporates among the alpine flowers.

My body relaxes to the rhythm, and
my mind marvels at the journey with
all its surprises, sights, sounds, smells…
I stare at a hummingbird drinking from a
nearby feeder, but two soaring eagles
replace them in my reverie…

Oxford in Snow

Extraordinary Winter light, snow, ice, a chill so strong it pulls the
skin around our bones,

subduing, silencing expression and stinging our lips, searing them
in the sharp air;

warming drinks, seeping slowly into us; strange, dark tracks and
trails in the whiteness,

our footsteps planted firmly as we tread an unknown depth of
frozen ground;

chunks of ice floating in the waterway, where, on its mint-cake
surface, ducks skid and skate;

glossy narrow-boats sealed to the elements; each tree white-etched,
so well defined in the brightness;

and in the city, historic doorways and gazing gargoyles have seen all
this before;

college spires, red chimneys climbing a deep blue sky, the sun gently
penetrates the atmosphere;

and later on, behind bare trees, it sinks, glowing low as we share our
wintry thoughts and notions.

Hilary Hughes

Pain

Sorrow, Grief

The pain, suffering and grief which Hilary has experienced, along with the struggles of others are represented here. There is a rawness about life; questioning, frustration, exhaustion – especially in an extended period of sleepless nights. Earlier low self-esteem and the power of a manipulative parent are evident. The fine line between life and death haunt the writer but also draw her closer to God.

Waking Nightmare

From out of nowhere they come: dark, winged shadows,
swooping down and into my head, barbing my path
to calm or rest; I can't control or fight as they torture,
tease, twist and turn my terrified mind;

invasions collide, clash vivid red and flashing white
in the blackness; I can't endure the endless onslaught
of the unseen, crashing waves, but I have to –
they have their own power;

hours pass, armies press on in battle, fizzing, popping,
blasting their way through – a series of explosions;
'Please don't!'; I can't go back; my heart cannot beat
to keep up with the frenzy of the fire;

my brain is burned in an electric storm;
again, again, a chaotic cacophony of sound – ugly,
cruel, bursting across my head from every direction,
stabbing my soul relentlessly hour after hour;

I reach out for hope but the sharp
pressure-wires prevent my release.

At last,

when conflict lessens, and time, such a time is spent,
and I am charred, scarred and numbed,
one insignificant thought takes hold,
tentatively, and leads into a space in which to hide,
until the horror begins once more…

Oh Sleep, Where art Thou?

Sleep,
the residual act of… falling
(wow! what a sensation!)
asleep… asleep… perchance to…
wake…
'Oh what a nuisance!' is the lighter side
of the experience, but even as I sense
a kind of relaxing, a nerve jars and
wakes the muscles. I wish… I pray…
I plead. I'm tired, exhausted,
yet… warm, cosy, comfortable,
breathing – rhythmic (almost) and reliable;
but brain says, 'Programme this slide,
this frame; change, connect, amalgamate,
turn and manoeuvre'; you can't forget
the complex thoughts and conversations,
tunes and heartbeats as you wait
for night to enclose your soul.
Sleep, that most desired healing
and rest for body and mind –
a state of calm, of aimless energies,
each dream emerging from the last –
illudes my nights; my troubled mind
is torn to shreds, from where, sometimes,
despite it all, deep in the desolate plains of time,
it slowly tips forward and drifts into…
sleep itself.

Heavy Heart

A dear friend diagnosed with inoperable cancer

As mucky snow melts
in a thin veil of rain,
our hearts drain empty of love,
washed around our brother;
he who weathered much,
embracing cold and heat,
walks now in death's shadow –
cast yet in light.

Deep drifts exist still
in gardens, on pavements,
reminders of winter's icy grip –
both surprising and depriving;
I wander in the damp and dusk,
asking, wondering
at the phases of our lives,
the unpredictability,
our search for pattern, order,
longing for value, love.

Lord, take this life,
in and through the hard-ness
and alone-ness,
and flood him still
with healing streams of strength
and joy and expectation,
that You will call him
when it's time,
in peace and confirmation
that his winter days are gone
with springtime's resurrection.

Nocturnal Nonsense

A flat battery and a limping chicken
A staircase in a forest
A risky business in the luggage trade
A purple ambulance screaming by
An angry vicar singing
A failure to play by the rules
A red ribbon for a brave act
A doubly incontinent woman and her dog
A cheeky sailor on the Tube
An ash tree growing through the ceiling
An ancient storm in a modern teacup
A calendar clock
A dream of an endless journey
A child's eyes through a frosty window
A woven Christmas star, forgotten
A debt that drags on and down
A glowing heart, a smiling face
All in my mind's strange pattern
Or un-pattern; I look for connections
And find contradictions and nod in the
Puzzling randomness of half-sleep, when awake.

Winter Song

Now is the winter of our discontent…
Contentment seems to lie so small or shallow
in our wintry minds; it is measured by the weather,
the cold, the change of plans or time, by the strength
or health we have or by long-held inhibitions,
prohibitions even, which wrestle with emotions,
causing sorrow, pain or doubt.

This season now has brought us such;
we weep with those who are bereft, in grief and
those who struggle on and even with ourselves, who,
paralysed by fear and sickness, float in a kind of
empty world. But, all around, unseen and yet alive
are those who pray and wait with us, poised in hope,
and with each dawn, a word to melt and thaw our frozen
existence; they weave a thread or two of warmth and gather
our misgivings, interpretations, expressions into
a shawl of comfort in which we wrap ourselves.

No room for complacency in our protection
and security but, with frosted glass our vision,
we deepen and maintain our trust in Him, who,
in true focus enables us to be at one –
with Him and so with all our family, releasing
the icy grasp of loss, embracing liberty;
making this winter warm with love, despite
the wind and wildness; remembering we can
cry and moan and laugh and shout and, under
the bridge that towers above the silent river,
mark this time for making memories, matching,
melding our new contentment in its winter…

No Swim

Remembering

'can't do swimming today, Miss,' (in hushed tones amidst the
    echoes of the pool)

verucca...
verucca...
period, Miss...
period...
verucca...
verucca...
athlete's foot...
cold...
verucca...
period...
...
...
...
(I'm saying)
period...

(but really I'm **SO** scared of the water, the deep, the drowning, the
    derisions... and I'm so disappointed, so disgusted with myself.
    The real reason I can't swim is not because of a period but
    because of my intense fear! That's the reason.)

Night-time

Loud,
out loud,
I want to scream
but cannot.
Years of suppressed
expression thwart
the purpose and the
manner of my yearning.
Deaf ears haven't heard
in any case.
My thoughts and passions
curled up tight like
a Catherine wheel,
which, if lit, would
spark and spiral,
shower and cascade,
whistle and squeal;
but
Silence.
I swallow, breathe
and press on.

Voices in my Head

in a younger life

No-one likes you,
no-one is interested.
You're weird,
you have to re-invent yourself.
They're not looking at you
(you're not worth it)
but they're judging you.
Something good happened,
so now, lots of bad things will happen.
You'll never be free of worry
and heaviness and bad things.
Life is like this, good things
happen to other people.
No-one will ever understand you,
believe you, believe in you.

mid-way

Don't hope for better, you're going to die soon.
You'll never escape your mother's control,
so it's no use trying to run away.
You can't dance any more, everyone
will look at you and you'll be embarrassed.
This (good feeling) won't last long,
something bad is going to happen very soon.
You can't hold up a hymn book, I won't let you,
you'll shake and tremble and sweat and run away.
No-one really likes you.
When you're (driving) on the road, you must jump
over the shadows, otherwise you're not good enough.

in an older life

There must be a way out of this hell.
I cry out to God, to anyone.
It's as if I'm being flung
about in a floating bubble,
no sense of time, position, space.
I can't stand or sit or steady myself.
I close my eyes.
I open them again.
There's no difference.
I imagine an ordinary life,
an ordinary dream
and it's ordered, yet comfortable,
characterful, colourful.
Now, it's chaotic, manic, electric,
hot-wired through my brain.
I want to shout and scream, "STOP!"
but I can't.

Because I'll wake people.

Crushed

Running away, running away.
A row of teeth, stained with blood;

fear, panic and pain rise from my stomach,
I find it hard to breathe;
I open my mouth but cannot speak,
sounds, disconnected from each other
suffocate themselves before they can be heard.
I want to run, but am fixed to the ground;
I feel sick and my eyes stare into space,
my jaw is clenched tight.
Dread, disgust and disappointment
thread their way into my head and heart;

I cannot tell where I am, momentarily paralysed.
Anger, then, and a sense of injustice flood in
and grip me like a vice. I cannot take a step.
When at last a restless calm, a choking breath
issues a space within calamity,
it is then possible to cry and weep,
for myself, yet not only me, but all those
hurt by her destructive fangs.
(Yet she is actually destroying herself.)
I've been running away from her
most of my life, but can I ever be free?

The Floods

Bangkok, November 2011

As water walls surge and saturate, search for space, contaminate,
I in my secret fragile state look on, confused, frustrated, willing
something to be done. Sometimes the flood abates, revealing
a rotten revulsion of what once was: decomposition of any natural
elements, and the pathos of an upturned plastic chair, floating,
out of reach;

then, another gate spills out a rush, a tide, into the liquid mass,
and then another – all converge and raise the river higher,
undaunted, determined to invade. What is this horror?
How did it happen? Where will it end, or when?

A thousand questions on the lips of frightened bankside dwellers
as they seek shelter, abandoning their flimsy shop-houses for
comparative safety of a 'storeyed' block; to wait and dry until…

My own instability, emotions, run deep, pulled in all directions
by care and love and duty, holding on to whatever I can
to stop myself from drowning…

Hilary Hughes

Muse

Faith, Love, Contemplation

Comment, imagination and an askance look at life are featured in these poems. There is a twinkle in the eye, a smile and a spring in the step as we wander through this section; an embracing of God's goodness and amazing creativity. Some pieces look back, others look to the future and to Heaven. Perceptions from the everyday and about specific situations blend with more dreamy pieces and about Writing itself.

I Leave Prayer Alone

I leave prayer alone.
I say, 'Everything's alright,'
And You look on
With Your smile.
I've got my day,
I've got my work,
I've got my plans,
And that's how I am.

But You can't stop loving me,
No, You can't stop loving me,
No, You won't stop loving me,
Why?

I ignore my friend's cry;
I busy myself with life
And pretend You don't know.
I've got to go,
I've got to get,
I've got to try,
And You don't get a look in.

But You can't stop loving me,
No, You can't stop loving me,
No, You won't stop loving me,
Why?

In case You heard
(Of course You did),
You've been listening all the time.
Why am I so slow to know
You never leave my side?

'Cos You can't stop loving me,
No, You can't stop loving me,
No, You won't stop loving me,
Why? Every parent knows.

What is Heaven Like?

We need not hope, for everything is certain;
I cannot fear, for I am in safe hands.
The ultimate destination;
no act of determination
can bring you here; it's just because you can…

…and do, choose life and love for constant inspiration,
to honour Christ, His heart your imitation;
and so, I pause to wonder,
what kind of place, or state,
might I expect, when welcomed into Heaven?

Will it be an urban or a rural situation?
Are there faces I remember that fulfil my expectation?
Might we run, or dance, or sing…
…drink wine and feed each other?
How might we pass the time? Or does that really matter?

I'd love to greet my father and remember
how much he wanted peace and consolation;
greet others too – catch up on conversation;
and wander over hills of grace, and swim
in tides of joy and new elation.

Riding horseback in the wind, breathing air's pure fragrance
and acknowledging a Saviour's degradation.
His light infuse your soul
and love burn in your heart
and with these thoughts enact your celebration!

What's Heaven like? No fear, no pain,
no need for justice or persuasion.
A uniquely special and a perfect vibe.
And so I know I must do more trusting;
pressing on, let's wonder at
the powerful truth that is our transformation.

Sleep

Started on a new medication

Hello, strange bedfellow,
so we meet, at last!
So often we have greeted,
then turned away, contact denied…

Nights passed, and you and I
endured an awkward conversation,
never knowing how the other might
behave. Where was the sense in that?
Overwhelmed by lack of rest, I struggled on,
but we did not agree.

Oh you and I,
we had a lot to wrestle with:
anger, hurt, anxiety, unease,
terrors of the mind and
anguish of the heart.
When we agreed, such peace and relaxation,
but before too long that
stormy pattern overcame our rights.

United, we can linger
in the land of imagination,
divided, fail to play out
aspects of our journey
set to mould the future with the past.

So, now we have an opening,
a chance to share a freedom,
a time and space so previously denied.
Can calm meet calm
in act of seamless beauty?
May we lie down together
in the comfort of the night?

Shall we agree, that now's the time
for shattering history's domination,
considering dreams and stillness
as our right and present state?

So, we wait, together, hoping
and believing that our treasure is
in sight. Night falls, curtains hiding time,
and we lay down together,
and you, sleep, and I
unite.

Honey Cookie Prayer

A dream of sight and taste,
Something good for others:
Sift the seasoned scripture
As a prayer base;
Cream deep desires
With pools of forgiveness;
Add some Holy Spirit to bind
Verses to my thoughts and actions;
Mix all together and divide
Into portions of intercession
And servanthood;
Leave time for change
Of colour and consistency.
Wait and wonder and believe
That new creation will emerge to be
Applied and tasted and approved
By God, the chef of sweet delight!

Meanderings and Wonderings

Does a star, that distant, distant heavenly body,
really have those pointed features, bursting out
in all directions, like a giant sparkler?

Does that star, a tiny jewel as we see it, and standing alone
from its astral neighbours by a million miles, burn itself out
before we spot it in sky's darkness?

That star, scattered into space as glitter-dust,
far beyond our time, this time, by those hands
who thought of us before our mothers knew;
a symbol of our being, one amongst a thousand thousand,
is known by God, as precious and important as all the rest;

He chose and counted in a star from one generation,
to lead, to lend a light to those who sought a king;
and now, He chooses me, not deserving or discerning
but out of passion for my soul; He says, 'Forgive;
I have forgiven you, and I will shine silver and gold,
ever pulsing in your universe!'

Does a star, dazzling in its own dimension,
look down and see me, glowing with His grace
as I turn in joy to meet and make a constellation?

Clouds

I wish I could name the clouds as they
roll above and around us each day.
Parallel lines of streaks and trails.
Purple furrows ploughed into the heavens.
Pelmets of velvet and gold to frame the hour.

A chaotic swirl, windblown, wispy;
a spreading band of cirrus plumes,
looming above the trees and houses.
In a winter sunrise, in the darkness,
iridescent, pastel vapours are lit
by the waking sun.

Turrets and tendrils turn our gaze as
we wonder at height, colour, movement.
Mirroring our lives, they change,
transform, amaze and frighten.
Tomorrow sweeps in and shapes
and shades us. Light illudes, allures,
defies, defines the cloud formations.

Up beyond our gaze, moving moisture
gathers, then drifts, descends into depths of
valleys, inverting itself: sky and earth
in a meeting place; a shroud, blanketing
our landscape; voluminous veils wave
and scatter, retreating to the heavens.

Constant change. Resolute remains.
The bizarre, the beauty beckoning the blue.

To a Child Born on my Birthday

Open your eyes and look beyond horizons,
seek out time with both your parents; enjoy them
and encourage them, as they, I hope, would do for you.
Let people be drawn to you by your self-assuredness and love.

Make-believe sometimes, but always try to know yourself –
think and speak from your identity, giving others cause
to be grateful and glad to be alive.
Trust someone to share the scared-ness and shame;
walk the talk of faith and try to be consistent, but,
be real within your head and heart and be prepared to fail.

Approval comes from God, his stamp is on you,
so beware of attainment for its own sake.
Sing and dance and celebrate, give time for true expression;
then take others by the hand and lead them gently,
not in a superior way, but one that says:
'We'll walk our road together';

be lost and found, be early, late and neither;
listen often, speak much less;
don't search for something that's already there.
Separation of the sacred and the secular sometimes is secret,
and mostly denies others of His care and love.

Your heart and spirit, mind and body aren't your own;
accept the price was paid and be free to live and grow;
discover and rediscover life and love;
forgiveness is a fragile cloak but you should try to wear it,
and, finding new patterns, follow and forget the hurt
and repossess this life which here on Earth
does not last forever; to make your mark is wonderful
but doesn't buy you peace, so stress not and be yourself
till the horizon comes.

Please Help Keep our Church Open

Low Mill, Farndale

Where in our lives does this place stand?
Is it a building, a focus, an awkward reminder,
a place of sadness or forgotten dreams?
a place of rest for our forbears, a venue for a season,
now discarded, disregarded, discouragingly disrespected?

Once anthems rose from organ pipes and voices,
deep with reverence and awe, breathing in the remnants
of incense, pollen and the dust of years,
breathing out the beauty of creation and the love of God;
rafters trembled with the resonance of sound, mice
scuttled out of sight and spiders hung suspended in the moment;

doors unlocked, all can enter in the gloom, a splinter shaft
of light through bluish pane illuminates the nave,
and chancel too is shrouded in a misty veil as darkness fades in part;
what function does this space allow? are all welcome?
stranger, robber, sullen teenager? widow in the night?
or only those whose coins slip into a rusty lid?

This polite request, this honest pleading, who is it who asks?
the valley folk, the historians round here?
to admire the lofty grandeur of the space,
the signs and secrets of the years,
the spire, the altar and the coloured glass;
is that desired, prioritised? perpetuation for its sake?
posterity goes stale with lack of interest or concern;

each stone, each timber, eroding, warping, infinitesimally,
    imperceptively,
and each slate slowly, slowly slipping from its grasp upon the past,
no part can ultimately stay the same, a grave or tombstone wears
    away
all through years and centuries, though it seems it's set to last;

a hymnal scatters brittle paper pages in the dust,
nativity straw stamped into a corner long ago;
an old umbrella, perhaps once green, spokes pointing
towards the ancient font, betrays the pleaders
and peeling paint, patched before, belies a constancy of care;
farmers' families and miners, shepherds, smelters, all were here,
lives measured by the seasons and sacraments, blossom and stove,
sand and straw, cinders and mud, tears of joy and of sadness
all combine in the mix of memories which make this place
a memorial to the past, the rhythm of life and death, scandals and
    surprises;

but what of now? who remain the faithful or the lost?
church and chapel then co-existing in an awkward way,
a belonging and believing thread twisted and twirled into a
prolonged, protracted history. The potential community
of church lies beyond, around this building – it may be used
to meet and pray and sing and worship but is its purpose –
to turn people to God, still in the sign that says:
'Please Help Keep Our Church Open'…?

Admirable, perhaps, but why? and how?
It may be that we ourselves should state,
'Please keep channels of communication open,
as we seek to be the living stones that build His church today,
both in this place, its heart in natural landscape, and in the suburbs
of the city and in all relationships we ever have and are.'

Close, lock and neglect this stone edifice, and in time,
no-one will remember who or why or when; they may wonder
still; so shall we know every place is a sacred space
as we give thanks to God and for the builders and designers
now gone, and for their children, scattered,
far from this valley and the sunshine butter yellow
that brought us here and so to read the sign,
'PLEASE HELP KEEP OUR CHURCH OPEN'.

Heaven Touches as we Breathe and Move

Such a fine line between life and death…
the very dryness of that state, the space
where the spiritual is so ordinary,
yet the ordinary is so spiritual.

Hello… goodbye, scarcely a whisper…
Heaven meeting Earth… is Heaven so near?

A presence, more than a shape-filled space,
floats on the tide, here… then gone;
a person goes about their life, their track
in parallel. Without realising, we tread
so close so often; never a chasm –
sometimes a small crack, a fissure, appears
and weakens the hold we think we have on life.

Breaths are breathed when body's core is stilled
and mind is with the angels; time marks duties,
weather changes, a pulse slows, skin pales,
the moon smiles while the sun sleeps
and a heart beats over that fine, thin line;
one more breath… the wind blows;
death releases its grip and life resumes;
lips moistened; the divine momentarily touched
the everyday. Earth glimpsed Heaven enough
to trust the place and life beyond;
sometimes the hold we think we have on life
sits astride that spider-silky thread and waits…

Goodbye… hello… almost a whisper…
the sweet sigh of recognition passes through
the sour sigh of regret… such a fine line…

Funny

Funny, how we try to stand out/blend in
according to our mood and situation;
tone, register, register, tone, modified and melded.
Do I speak to the cat like I do to my students?
Do they make their reply with what I want to hear?

The curtains are drawn till the morning;
when pulled back, they reveal the new day;
behind them at night, we can only imagine
the bonds and the conflict sealed or unleashed,
which in daytime become so ordinarily
tempered, even vague in expression.

Open-mindedness, self worth and sympathy
assert themselves, slowly, so we discern
when to blend in and when to stand out;
our own peculiar selves are carving
an intriguing path deep in the canyons of life
and we learn our place and position.

My students say, 'Hi' to the cat and all
makes sense… for now…

The Door

Revelation 3:20; John 10:1-10; Song of Songs 5:2

The door, a door, opens into a space or closes it away.
The door fits in its frame and, by a gentle turn,
swings in its plane, outwards, inwards.
It is a symbol of invitation, exclusion,
of status, of welcome. Behind it – the world,
the 'outside', the heat, the storm, the anguish of life.

From outside to inside is but a knock, a push,
a key to reveal a space of freedom, of light,
of warmth, security. As You stand at my door,
have I closed it against You? Do I think
my secrets are hidden from You?
The choices, the fun, the dreams and plans
I think You might take from me, keep me
from rushing to open the door at the slightest tap.

The Lover sleeps, but her heart is awake,
listening for the knock of her lover,
when, heart pounding, she longs for
the moment she'll see him again.

Rooms have doors, for protection,
demarcation, privacy, partying;
But, oh Lord, nothing can separate me from You;
Jonah-like I may conceal myself in some dark,
draughty passage, but You keep on knocking,
and lovingly wait for me to reach for the handle
and wrench it open. And the outside becomes
inside and I am at home with You.

The Envelope

Its contents secret, slipped silently inside,
Now a flat white rectangle, its shapely folds
Stuck down, sealed, waiting. What clues reveal
Its mission, its sender or its purpose?

Is it to impart news, crucial, inconsequential?
To encourage, damage, gossip or deceive?
Love's declaration, examination, intention?
Demanding payment or threat of eviction?

There are none. Only a faint grey mark, its
Origins unclear. Its destination the only certainty.
Who is to receive it? Colleague, cousin, lover?
Tenant, student, occupier? Friend or brother?

And what result, reaction may follow its unravelling?
Humour, despair, ugly thoughts of recrimination?
Delight, excitement or the silence of resignation?
Such a small, thin parcel of mysterious worth, yet
Such power to confirm, deny or meet some expectation.

The German 'Umschlag' sounds as if it gives permission
For tearing, unsealing, to allow its revelation.
The English (or the French) seems so prim and private.
If no one opens it…

Orbit

For a friend

When the world stops making sense,
sometimes faith and fear walk hand in hand;
but God's mercy never runs dry.

We cling to Christ, but also what we know can happen;
His victorious love reaches out and over us
and over what we fear;

this we take on trust; these awkward ones,
fear and faith, stride on, or sometimes, tiptoe;
our hearts and minds, our bodies, weary
from the travelling, unravelling the evidence,
yet with assurance of His will.
God's mercy never runs dry.

Because our faith is neither paralytic hope,
nor wishful thinking, (though if truth be known,
it sometimes seems that way!)
we want a confident declaring that
God will help our unbelief and put our
worries into reasonable perspective;

for we pray to Him who healed, yet suffered too,
and because He made us and knows us perfectly.
He takes our faith in one hand, our fear
in the other, and we are safe and smiling.
God's mercy never runs dry.

Because Christ stands in the gap, we make sense
of the world, and we are blessed.

Amen. (I pray this with you)

Back Doors of the Van

Who do you say that I am?
'You're everything to me',
'You're my salvation' –
Are those my words,
or someone else's?
Have I forgotten who You are,
or who I am in You?

On the back doors of a van:
two pictures – a 'before' and 'after';
after a deep clean, the second picture's
bright and new-looking; but… here, a scar,
a scratch, betrays that truth, and the
picture does not advertise the product,
however many times it's seen.

I want to trust You, Lord, but
deny myself the opportunity because
I look away, to tasks I 'have' to do,
to the 'honour' I seek for myself,
even unintentionally, by 'doing',
'being' a certain way; I do not
appreciate the destitution of my soul.

My mother's life, over now,
her body is a box of ash.
I'll take nothing with me when I leave,
as I came in with nothing.
How sick am I to think that I
am anything at all? But, I can
be anything in You, with You,
for You, because Your time, Your plan
transcends these 'earthly' thoughts.

As days go by, You subtly speak into my heart;
You make me face up to my irresponsibility.
Life is for living, death for dying;
yet the fine line between the two is always
present in my mind. Lord, I'm looking at You,
just looking at You; I need You, I'm lost without You.

Be my 'before', my 'after', but always my
forgiving friend, reminding me of
my freedom… from the back doors of a van.

Rescue

After the Writers' Day, London

Today I read the signs, listened, ended up going in the right
  direction;
reached my destination; by grace You showed me who I am
and how I can be faithful and productive, alive and influential;

old music, stale, transformed into vibrancy and efficacy.
The world is vast, so vast, and we all have our view of it;
my perspective coloured by my life but also by my Maker
and all of His creation. Laws, skills, revealed in different ways.

There is such warmth and beauty in life and in relationships,
but there is also such injustice and failure.
Name them, unfold and declare them, revive and restore them,
and listen! Hide sometimes, but then break out, and feel
the sun, the rain, the dust, the pain and… write!

Hilary Hughes

Hit the Ground Running

Leaf-hopping frog dives then, deeply;
Canyon-swooping bird snatches then, quickly;
Hill-roaming pony canters then, wildly;
Ocean-hunting seal circles then, crazily;

All these and more remind me of myself,
I'm never still, rarely satisfied, always
Searching, seeking, reasoning,
Smacking myself in the face!

How can I get there yesterday
Instead of enjoying here, today?
Value depends on velocity… but,
No, that's a lie. I'm running, now,
Not away, but towards my future,
Whatever, wherever that is.

My knees are scraped, head pounds,
Feet ache and vision blurred.
I pray and offer myself again,
Me and my big mouth and messy life.

I think I can protect myself – I laugh!
But I can allow His work in me.
Don't want to count success
As tasks done or battles won, just that
Relationships may grow and flourish.

And as I move and breathe, as I love
And as I write, may each element and
Dimension be alive with hope and
Beauty and forgiveness. Don't run,
Woman! Slow down, believe, belong,
Receive His peace and promise,
Then... fly!

People

Friends, Family, Strangers

A confessed 'people-watcher', Hilary observes groups and individuals, known and unknown, real and imaginary. The death of a friend and the impact this has on family and community is profound. Here we also catch the joy of having longed-for children as we read 'A Son' and 'Baby Girl'. Hilary tries to get under the skin of the victims in difficult/tragic situations. People often leave a deep impression. This is true of her mother, whom Hilary has to put in God's hands. Finally she pays tribute to her father, whom she only truly got to know as he was dying.

Travellers' Tales

Three stout gents sit snug,
safe from the cold windy platform,
unruly hair shaking
as they compare train numbers…

Sales reps taking calls on Blackberries,
on the move – cancel this, amend that, email them…
Time, stretched between stations, incognito,
unassuming and assuming,
a no-one, a someone;
The Times, the Sun, the brie baguette,
the crumpled sandwich;
distances and destinations
determined on a flimsy orange card…
Listening to… anything.
(No-one knows my iPod;
turn it up.
I'm in Venezuela;
turn it down…)
A traveller with a lived-in look
advises a friend on her love life,
or lack of it…

The effervescence of a black nurse
cursing sensational headlines
about the NHS;
sleepy mongrel hiding
between the seats,
tired tail, lying still in the aisle;
feelings – freedom – from work, life,
who I am or need to be,
from home, demands;
neither child nor sister, wife nor mother;
a traveller, an anonymous passenger,

changing seats, transferring trains,
extracting luggage, sipping steamed milk
with cinnamon from a cardboard cup;
waiting and wondering and hoping,
in suspension – neither here, nor there,
in transition; while in motion I am
whoever I want to be, whatever
I am prepared to be;
North – nearer,
South – slower,
East – endless,
West – wandering.

In the early winter evening,
shadows flicker through the dusty window;
rumbling, shaking, dragging,
hissing, humming;
accents, tongues, merge and emerge…

Seat-back pyramid parallel patterns,
interlocking squares, stripes,
thick and thin, blue, green and black –
some order in the travel;
heart tugged, tugged towards
the terminus of reality,
who I must be, what I must do…

Valentine's Day

A dear friend has a critical operation

Over all the earth You reign,
And over a bed in ICU
Your design shapes surgeon's skill
And monitoring machine.
A thousand unseen beings
Guard the room and whisper
Your gracious presence.
Caring hands protect
And watchful eyes check
A myriad of tiny movements
Only you can know.
With Your light, Your hope,
A community holds its breath
And stands and sits
And kneels and waits
In awe of You and
What You will do today
And in the coming days for him.

He Dies

To his wife

At ocean's darkened shore we stand
and watch the ship on far horizon;
the daylight dawns and she has
disappeared from view;
the stones beneath our feet
seem hard and cold as
we shiver in the chilly morning;

stepping back from you a little
as you end your vigil…
the wondering and whispering of God's
governance and intervention,
of His intention to transport
your nearest and dearest, dearest friend
to rest (an end to the ravage of
that merciless disease) is,
and will be, yours and yours to keep.

We cannot, perhaps will not,
understand the journey we have taken;
and you, whose heart is broken,
most of all, we care for and
will never let you be forsaken,
neither our loved one be forgotten
but remembered always as a friend –
His friend, your friend and life's
companion – and as the tide ebbs
and flows and the night stars pulse
with light, shards of life sill strew
themselves across the sand.

May life's rhythms return
and give you sleep and rest...

A Son

deep dark eyes, bright as polished blackwood –
the windows to an as yet unknown soul,
you smile at me as much as anyone, and stand
quite firmly on my knee with your splayed toes
and stare and smile again; my first moments
with my new child; he plays with the twisted ties
on my Indian dress and I try to take it in;

just hours ago I stood alone, and sank to the hard floor
and prostrate, lay before the Lord and moaned,
'if you don't want this for me Lord, then that's okay,
but please, please take my heartache away.'
and then the post box clanged, a daily sound,
but something brought me to my feet and made
me retrieve the letters lying there…

a common, non-descript brown envelope,
I wondered at its contents, hardly hoped
for news; but there it was: 'an Anglo-Asian boy,
just five months old, to visit and consider, please phone…'
I read and read again, overcome with, well,
with joy and fear and shock and a wave of longing
just to be there, see him, touch him, know him;

and there I was, in a kind, safe home, meeting
foster parents and discussing his short life
lived so far within the care of this family,
but soon to change and to unite with ours,
in our home, our church, our wider family too;
and next we chased a rapid gathering of things:
pushchair, bottles, nappies and not-so-tiny clothes;

and so began our life, no longer grieving
but receiving such precious, precious moments
with our son; he slept and fed so calmly and so well,
he chuckled at all sorts of things, played the keys
of our piano with excitement, we could hardly
take it in; tangle of black curls, sienna skin,
shrieks of delight at the sound of bath taps...

how extraordinary; a gift, desired, yes, but not
expected in this way; what trials and frustrations
lay ahead we did not know; we just so celebrated him
and tried as best we could to give him love and help
him find his way; his bright eyes lighting up with
every rhythm, every note of music played, as if to say,
'music is my second breath, I will absorb it always...'

Tsunami Girl

Her gaze is towards the ocean – flatness, mud and floating leaves.
Quiet. Bird takes off, metal clashes on metal. Quiet. Too quiet.
Brothers, fathers, cousins. When? How? Where? Find them, ever?
Salt and sewage smell in her mouth. Dirt and steam and death.

Alone, a girl – isolation on the step of a broken house.
And again a trembling, shaking, sifting sand and wood,
gasping, choking, panic looming near. Then, a settling.
Shaking, is it the ground or her that's shaking, shaking?
Her arms pulled and squeezed round her as if to tie her still.

Reccuring vision of a rolling, angry wave and blackness,
a tightness and a blindness in a waking nightmare.
Screams and wails from unnamed voices, faces, known before
and now secreted away, somewhere, she may never know.

Sweat gathers in her mask, can she breathe once more?
Swallowing and swallowing to push the fear away,
if there is a God here or anywhere, she pleads with him to stay.
Last year she fell as rocks rumbled, but, not like this;

in shock and yet with, somehow, acceptance, she bends
to pick up bits from the damp and mangled mess
to make a nest until the care she pleads for comes,
and life, a changed one, resumes amidst the wreckage.

Home from Home[1]

You're on another level
above, beyond the clouds,
soaring to an altitude remote,
removed from commonplace of time;
freed for now, from fear, from pain,
from those burdens laid upon you over years,
and, as you race across the sea, and over land,
the distance grows, as does the sense of liberation;
mountains peek through clouds and
velvet night reveals the palest dawn,
and with this, a present future, beautiful,
reflective, loving, giving, purpose, value.

As you descend and discern shapes
and signs of life, the new level offers
passion, compassion, excitement,
acceptance, and, inhaling those first
few breaths of humid air, I see you smile.

---

[1] The person referred to in this poem confirmed these sentiments months later, before he heard the poem, as he told me how he felt the day he travelled and then arrived in Asia.

Baby Girl

'Baby girl' – that pink fluffy phrase – now beautiful... real;
I gaze on her, lying beside me; I'm exhausted, it's happened,
she's here.

When first told I was pregnant I could not take it in and still cannot
now, while slowly, all sickness and pain from the pushing subsides
as she sleeps.

Having her, holding her, feeding and changing her, feeling that
    incredible
joy yet awesome responsibility – seems like a dream, and will for a
long time yet.

Our family – longed for, prayed for – celebrates our completeness:
our miracle, darling adopted son now has a home-grown sister.
And I have a miracle daughter.

Shame on the Streets

Written after the riots in London, Birmingham and elsewhere in August 2011

smash	belonging, the power of the crowd	**surge**
shout	anger released and the passion of persuasion	**signal**
run	no care for consequences	**stone**
grab	just join in, become part of the thrill, the chase	**move, now**
text	we want, we want, we want – what do we want?	**follow**

we want to be loved, to be trusted, to have hope,
to be shown how much we have; we know
only hate and anger, desperate defiance;

millions starve and suffer, moaning in the heat,
all that not-sensed, forgotten injustice;

the cry is that they can't have what they want,
ruthless rebellion, reckless fighting,
violent vandalism, inciting, exciting;

smash	bottles, bricks bombard a bank and break the steely face of order and authority	**surge**
shout	where this leads is not considered; mobs and masks and mugging meld into a movement	**signal**
run	no waiting, choosing, paying; take possession, snatch, grip, loot at random	**stone**
grab	a momentary muse on what might happen later intercepted by the weight and the power of the night	**move, now**

text guilt or fear of punishment fades, **follow**
chaotic confusion quells remorse,
responsibility

unashamed, untamed, they riot on;
then, one of them is bruised or burned,
and, abandoned by the rest,
cries out in blame,
'It's their fault!'
a message comes, rapid, revolutionary –
habit responds without a thought,
a riot's born and blazes on…

tomorrow – crushed cans, lager licked by straying dogs;
glass and stones and boxes strewn across a wind-blown street;
a cordon and a truck and helmets of police;
and an eerie quiet reigns in the wake of today;
shrieking, swearing, whispers, tears, behind their doors,
they're not the same, part of something past, now gone;
what's new? the power of possibility – but whose hands
hold the key? the crowd… the streets… belonging…

shout… follow…

Riots

a thread woven deep into the fabric of the night,
to 'bare shops and smash the feds'
surprises middle class suburbia
but so does the thread which follows
to 'regain the streets and clean up'

———————

an expression of identity:
we've been ignored,
we resent that,
they refuse to look at us,
so we're alienated
and our hatred is fed;
we get hungry for riot,
like a fever, like a battle,
its energy, amazement, excitement;
powerful now, soon powerless…
who are we?

Hilary Hughes

Attempt at Suicide on the Line

Life.

A step too far…
the train, a regular into town
braked, just in time, and he fell,
in shock, between the rails,
shiny black shoes scattering stones,
and lay still, very still, as if he
could not believe his plan
had failed;

and then he cried,
cried because of everything,
and all the people standing there
and how he could have hurt them
too; and he wept while two policemen
lifted his body from the track,
his body from the track, his mind,
his mind still down there,
and yet, it wasn't, it was in
a dream from yesterday,
last night, this morning,
tearing at his skull, his throat
dry from panting, summoning
the will to jump, to jump, just
before the train entered the station.

Ash trees nodded from the bank on the
opposite platform, while the small
crowd round him shook their heads
in sad incomprehension; the sky,
already grey, its pallor almost ghostly,
ushered him into the white-bright
light of the waiting ambulance.

'What's your name, son?
What's your name?'
'What's my name?' he thought,
'I know my name, why don't they?'
'Is there anyone to call?'
'Irrelevant now,' he muttered.

Travellers wondered at the stranger,
why he'd come into their lives,
what would send him to this
desperate state, but then
moved on, away, distracted,
then, forgetting him entirely, swallowed
up with life, activity, responsibility;

and the man in the ambulance lay
in the ambulance, his black shoes,
so shiny, removed to the floor;

and the ambulance drew onto the road
where the man who had jumped,
the man with the black shiny shoes
had come from, and on to and into
the A and E that he'd left that morning
after his night shift, and had made his
way over the bridge to the railway track
to jump, to finish it all, regardless of
anything, anyone.

A step too near…
it seemed so now; his colleague,
frowning above him, saying, 'Hello Jim…'

and the delayed train rolled into town.

Life.

Peace Place

For a friend, who confirmed this as prophetic, in that it was a special place in relation to guidance for ministry

step
off the world and
lean
against the rough bark of an oak tree,
feel
its grooves beneath your fingers
breathe
the smell of the harvest on the breeze
hear
only a dog bark at a lone goose, as she flies above
let
panic subside, details depart, voices fade away
step
away from fear, from anger, guilt and duty
climb
into the branches, closer to the heart of nature
stay
and wait awhile, the world still turning
stop
sense the powerful love that God the Father shows you
take
and trust, knowing it is fully yours; as you
look
down across the valley,
see
a wide, relentless, racing river, but
notice
the quiet pools beside the rapids, before you
step
back in

Hilary Hughes

Waiting With Her

Written when our attempts to help our young disabled friend in Asia were thwarted

Are you who I think you are?
Neglected, vulnerable, weak, alone?
Have you deceived me in any way?
Should I rely on what you tell me?
Do you really know me or just
think you do, as I do you?

In the same world, yet worlds apart,
I felt drawn to you, as if I was going
to be part of your future, if I could.
You're determined, independent,
despite all you've been through,
but your past is still your present,
and your future – as what was done
cannot be undone.

And yet, and yet, I've felt a mission,
calling, responsibility, call it what
you will, to go beyond what's sensible,
what's 'Western', what's secure,
to see your potential, to give
what's been denied before,
to activate a change for you, in you,
with no strings attached;

but because of feelings, emotions
running high, I know I must be
careful not to let heart rule head –
neither mine nor yours,
but be prepared to show my love
by being firm and strong and patient,
awaiting your response; and if, in
the end, we cannot help each other
(for indeed you've already taught me much)
I'll pray for you forever and trust you to God
and thank Him for you, dear one.

Creation to Cremation

Death of Mother

When first you breathed and breathed and cried,
God already knew; you grew between the hills and mills,
your accent altered for want of better, greater things,
and so, to London, where you lived and loved and lost
and won again a truly gracious man, handsome in heart
as in looks; connected with the world of romance,
dance, film-stars and music – a comfort from
the wickedness of war.

But still a barrier – of insecurity and self – haunted
you and ate into your soul, so that connections
became sour, disconnected, bitter, melancholy;
this slowly burned away inside, isolating, dislocating
son from mother, daughter from father,
alienating friend and sister;

conversation coiled around you, paralysing our
attempts to love; absorption with appearance,
style and self-perpetuation impressed the world
but not ourselves. You stunned us into silence
with weighty words and painful wounds.

And then, as age bent you and exhausted you,
you settled into sleep and breathed your last,
your brain blooded, your heart and voice stilled,
your crumpled body, from which so much emanated,
now reduced to ash. God knew and knows.
When we could not love you...

Legacy

Remembering Dad

Funds, investments, gains, adjustments,
all of these remain, to claim, release or reinvest.
And it is helpful, thoughtful, too, that all the years
of toil created future wealth, but not for him.

Riches, words, deeds, examples,
handed down by generations, mean
that heavenly treasure now is ours to claim
and reinvest, to transfer to others, projects,
through awareness of the Spirit naturally
and of our deep devotion to our Master's call.
We plan, we trust, often we fail, but still
Love's legacy is ours, available at a moment's
notice and with no strings attached!

He did not really reap much dividend
from those long years, not in this earthly life.
But Heaven grants him freedom, riches, healing,
beyond measure; and I thank him for his blessing
and avow to do him proud and acknowledge I am loved,
and love and love until I join him there.

Contact the Author

Thank you for reading my poems and reflections. If you'd like to read more, see my Facebook page – Hilary Jane Hughes Creative Writer – and my website – **hit-the-ground-running.org** – or contact me via the website. Let me know what you think, please! I can visit groups or present work on a theme or at an event/service. Just let me know!

Hilary Jane Hughes

Similar Books from the Publisher

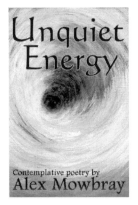

Unquiet Energy
Alex Mowbray

This inspiring book of contemplative poetry takes you on a journey through life, addressing the fragile nature of society and human life, asking difficult questions on the way, but often finding encouraging answers. Illustrated with beautiful full colour paintings by Ruth Griffin, Nicole Matthews and Alex Mowbray, this book makes an ideal gift.

In Short
Sue O'Donnell

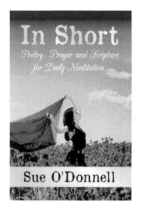

This heart-warming devotional was birthed out of Sue O'Donnell's daily journey with the Lord.

Perfect for daily readings and quiet meditation, these morsels of wisdom and worship will inspire and grow your own personal relationship with Jesus.

My Art of Poetry
Judy Edwards

Art and Poetry have been at the heart of Judy Edwards. This is expressed in this book by her love for nature, particularly from her home in the South West of England.

Books available from www.onwardsandupwards.org